Backyard Books

Are you a Bee?

KINGFISHER
LONDON & NEW YORK

Copyright © Kingfisher 2000
Text copyright © Judy Allen 2002

Published in the United States by Kingfisher,
175 Fifth Avenue, New York, NY 10010
Kingfisher is an imprint of Macmillan Children's Books, London.
All rights reserved.

Distributed in the U.S. by Macmillan, 175 Fifth Avenue, New York, NY 10010
Distributed in Canada by H.B. Fenn and Company Ltd., 34 Nixon Road, Bolton, Ontario L7E 1W2

Library of Congress Cataloging-in-Publication Data
Allen, Judy.
Are you a bee?/by Judy Allen; illustrated by Tudor Humphries.—1st ed.
p. cm.–(Backyard books)
1. Bees—Juvenile literature. [1. Bees.] I. Humphries, Tudor, ill. II. Title.
QL565.2.A44 2001
595.79'9–dc21   00-047814

ISBN 978-0-7534-5804-4

Kingfisher books are available for special promotions and premiums. For details contact:
Special Markets Department, Macmillan, 175 Fifth Avenue, New York, NY 10010.

For more information, please visit www.kingfisherbooks.com

Printed in China
8 10 9
8TR/0211/WKT/DIG(MA)/140MA

Backyard Books

Are You a Bee?

Judy Allen and Tudor Humphries

KINGFISHER
NEW YORK

Are you a bee?

Perhaps you are a honeybee.
If so, your mother is a queen.
She looks like this, and she
lays eggs.

Your life began inside one of her eggs.

When you hatch, you are not a pretty sight.

You are a larva.

You are in a small room with
six walls. It's called a cell.

Your older sisters bring food.
Eat it and grow.

Grow until you fill your cell.

One of your older sisters puts
a wax ceiling on your cell.

Inside your closed cell you change a lot.

When you are ready, chew a hole in the ceiling and climb out.

NOW you look like a bee.

You have a hairy body with stripes,
six legs, and four wings.
You have two feelers on your head.
You have a stinger.

You are not alone. You have
a few hundred brothers and
thousands of sisters.

You live in a nest built by
your older sisters.

Your nest might be in
a hollow tree.

It might hang down from
a tree branch.

Most likely it will
be inside a hive.

11

Your brothers
are drones.
They don't do much.

You and your sisters
are workers.
You do everything.

You clean the nest,
feed the larvae, take care of
the queen, and build new cells.

You fan the nest
with your wings to
cool it in the summer.

You guard the nest to keep
out strange bees.

Busy, busy, busy.

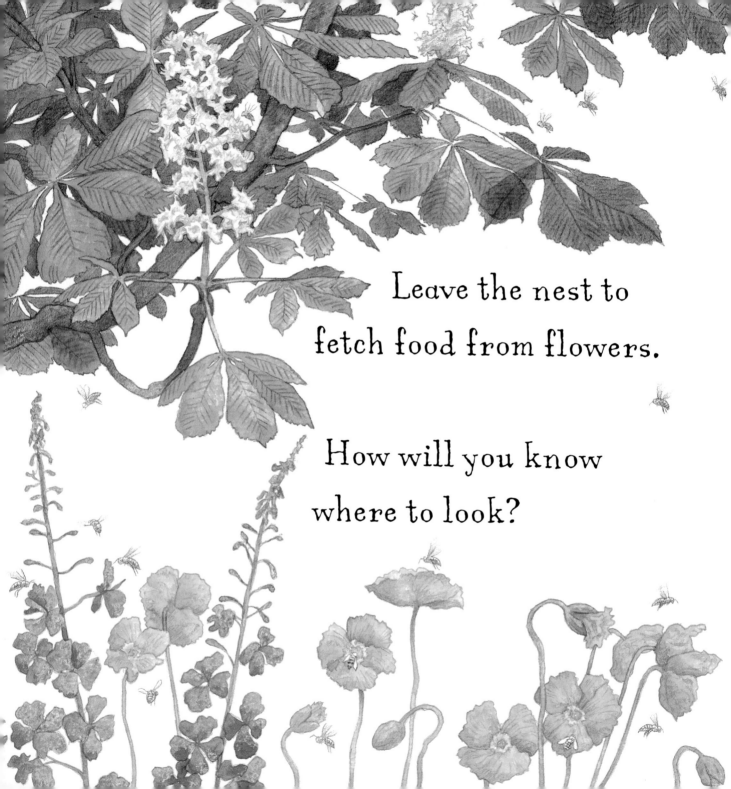

Leave the nest to
fetch food from flowers.

How will you know
where to look?

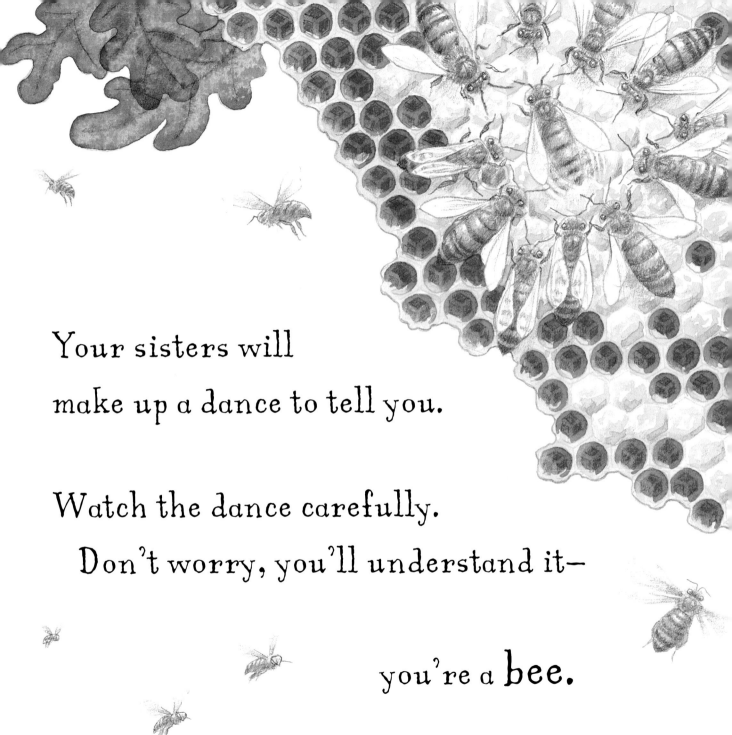

Your sisters will
make up a dance to tell you.

Watch the dance carefully.
Don't worry, you'll understand it—

you're a **bee.**

There is sweet liquid
in flowers. It's called
nectar, and it's hidden
deep inside. This is not
a problem. You have
a long tongue.
You
can
reach it.

You also have a special stomach to carry it in. You'll get pollen-dust all over you. Scrape it off with your front legs and put it in the pollen baskets on your back legs.

When you get home,
your sisters will help
you put the nectar and
the pollen into storage
cells. Mix some of the
nectar with pollen
to make beebread.

Leave the rest of the
nectar to turn into honey.

Beebread is good to eat.
So is honey.

If you find a new patch
of flowers, be sure to tell
your sisters.

How?
Dance, of course!

More eggs hatch.
More larvae turn into bees.
The nest gets very crowded.
What will happen next?

The old queen,
your mother, leaves.

She takes you and a lot
of your sisters with her.

Deep in the nest a royal larva is hatching. She is in a different kind of cell, and she is fed rich food called royal jelly. When she becomes a bee, she is a young queen.

She flies away and mates with drones from another nest so that she can lay eggs. When she flies home again, she will be the new queen.

21

Fly with your sisters—follow
the old queen.

Stay together—you are part of a swarm.
When the queen stops,
swarm around her.

Now you must build a new
nest. But where?

Maybe the queen will send
scout bees to find a good place.

Or maybe a beekeeper will find you and take you all to an empty hive.

Why is the beekeeper dressed like this?

In case you get flustered and try to sting.

However,

if your mother looks
a little like this   or this

or this

you are not a bee.

You are...

...a human child.

You do not have a hairy body
with stripes on it.

You do not have a long tongue.

You do not have a stinger.

It is very unlikely that you have hundreds of brothers and thousands of sisters.

But you can do a lot
of things that a bee can't do.

You can still eat bread and honey,
but you'll never have to fetch
your food from flowers.

Best of all,
you don't have
to be busy, busy,
busy all day long.

Did You Know...

...bees are happy to live in a hive, because the beekeeper has already built part of the nest for them. If bees live in a hollow tree, they have to build the whole nest themselves.

...a worker bee can sting only once, then it dies—but a queen bee can sting many times.

...bees carry pollen from flower to flower on their furry bodies. The pollen from one flower rubs off onto others and makes seeds, which will grow into new plants.

...the average worker bee makes one-and-a-half teaspoons of honey in her lifetime.